Magic, Myth, and Myst

DISCOVER

WEREWOLVES

DO YOU BELIEVE?

This series features creatures that excite our minds. They're magic. They're myth. They're mystery. They're also not real. They live in our stories.

45th Parallel Press

Published in the United States of America by Cherry Lake Publishing Group
Ann Arbor, Michigan
www.cherrylakepublishing.com

Reading Adviser: Beth Walker Gambro, MS Ed., Reading Consultant, Yorkville, IL
Book Design: Felicia Macheske

Photo Credits: © S-BELOV/Shutterstock.com, cover; © Stockimo/Shutterstock, 1; © welburnstuart/Shutterstock, 5; © Marcin Perkowski/Shutterstock, 7; © Semmick Photo/Shutterstock, 8; © Gleb Semenjuk/Shutterstock, 11; © Valentina Photos/Shutterstock, 12; © Martin Mecnarowski/Shutterstock, 15; © Vuk Kostic/Shutterstock, 17; © Pepgooner/Shutterstock, 21

Graphic Elements Throughout: © denniro/Shutterstock; © Libellule/Shutterstock; © sociologas/Shutterstock; © paprika/Shutterstock; © ilolab/Shutterstock; © Bruce Rolff/Shutterstock

45th Parallel Press is an imprint of Cherry Lake Publishing.

Library of Congress Cataloging-in-Publication Data

Names: Loh-Hagan, Virginia, author.
Title: Discover werewolves / Virginia Loh-Hagan.
Description: Ann Arbor, Michigan : Cherry Lake Publishing, [2023] | Series: Magic, myth, and mystery express | Audience: Grades 2-3 | Summary: "Will silver kill a werewolf? How does a person turn into a werewolf? Books in the Magic, Myth, and Mystery Express series for young readers explore spooky creatures that go bump in the night, fill our dreams (or nightmares!), and make us afraid of the dark. Written with a high-interest level to appeal to a more mature audience and a lower level of complexity, clear visuals help struggling readers along. Considerate text includes fascinating information and wild facts to hold readers' interest, and support comprehension. Includes table of contents, glossary with simplified pronunciations, and index"—Provided by publisher.
Identifiers: LCCN 2022039539 | ISBN 9781668919682 (hardcover) | ISBN 9781668920701 (paperback) | ISBN 9781668922033 (ebook) | ISBN 9781668923368 (pdf)
Subjects: LCSH: Werewolves—Juvenile literature. | Animals, Mythical—Juvenile literature.
Classification: LCC GR830.W4 L64 2023 | DDC 398.24/54—dc23/eng/20220826
LC record available at https://lccn.loc.gov/2022039539

Cherry Lake Publishing would like to acknowledge the work of the Partnership for 21st Century Learning, a network of Battelle for Kids. Please visit *http://www.battelleforkids.org/networks/p21* for more information.

Printed in the United States of America
Corporate Graphics

Dr. Virginia Loh-Hagan is an author, university professor, former classroom teacher, and curriculum designer. Her dogs howl at full moons, fireworks, postal workers, gardeners . . . the list goes on. She lives in San Diego with her very tall husband and very naughty dogs.

CONTENTS

CHAPTER ONE

Hairy and Howling

"Owoooo!" Werewolves are scary!

Werewolves are humans. These humans **shift**. Shift means to change.

New werewolves can't control themselves under a full moon.

SCIENCE

Some people are very hairy. This doesn't mean they're werewolves. They might have a rare condition. It makes people grow thick hair all over.

They change into wolves. They shift during full moons. Werewolves hunt. They kill. They feast.

Werewolves are **shapeshifters**. They change their shapes. They change their forms.

There are different types of shapeshifters. Some witches can turn into ravens.

Werewolves have human forms. They look like normal humans. Some may look different. Werewolves have wolf forms. They look like huge wolves.

If werewolves are cut when in human form, their wounds have fur in them.

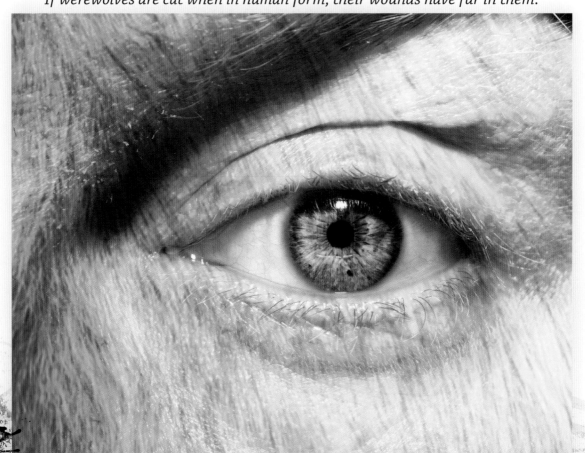

Did You KNOW?

A werewoman is a female shapeshifter. But she doesn't have to be a wolf. She can be any animal. She uses the same change process as a werewolf.

CHAPTER TWO

Beware of the Wolf Pack

Werewolves are **beasts**. A beast is a large animal or monster with four legs. They're powerful.

It is said that werewolves are stronger than polar bears.

They see well. They have **night vision**. They can see in the dark. Werewolves work as a **pack**. A pack is a wolf family. They talk. They howl.

Werewolves sense each other's pain and death.

Have You
HEARD?

Lykoi cats are called werewolf cats. They're named after the Greek word for wolf. They look like werewolves. Their fur is scraggly and patchy.

CHAPTER THREE

Slaying the Beasts

Werewolves have weaknesses. They hate silver. It won't kill werewolves. But it will hurt them. **Quicksilver** will kill them. It's liquid mercury. It's poison.

Like wolves, werewolves can be very secretive.

STAY SAFE!

- Stay in crowds! Werewolves stay away from crowds.

- Cover yourself in mud. This is so human smells don't reach the werewolf. Stay out of sight!

Werewolves hate vampires. They fight them. Many have died fighting vampires.

Many believe silver bullets will kill werewolves.

CHAPTER FOUR

Beastly Changes

There are different ways to become a werewolf.

Werewolves feed on humans. They bite. Some humans survive. These humans become werewolves.

Know the LINGO!

Alpha: leader of the pack

Lupine: sharing characteristics of a wolf

Skinwalkers: Native American word for shapeshifters

ORIGINS

There's a Greek story about werewolves. Zeus is a god. He visited King Lycaon. The king didn't believe he was Zeus. Zeus punished the king. He turned the king into a wolf. Lycaon may be the first werewolf.

Some are born as werewolves. They have 2 werewolf parents.

Turning into a werewolf is painful. Bones grow longer. They change shape. They move. Skin changes. Organs move around. Fur grows.

Different cultures have different beliefs about werewolves.

Real
WORLD

The Quileute are Native Americans. They live in Washington State. They were in the *Twilight* stories. They were shown as werewolves. Legend says their tribe started with wolves. Two wolves were turned into humans.

CONSIDER THIS!

Say What?

Read Torch Graphic Press's book *The Vampire and the Lost Locket* by Kate Tremaine. Explain werewolves' strengths and weaknesses. Which monster would win in a battle?

Think About It!

Some sources claim that silver kills werewolves. Other sources claim that silver only hurts werewolves. Why do you think there are such differences?

LEARN MORE

Peabody, Erin, and Victor Rivas. *Werewolves*. New York: Little Bee Books, 2017.

McCollum, Sean. *Werewolves: The Truth Behind History's Scariest Shape-Shifters*. Read by Various Narrators. Mankato, MN: Capstone Press, 2017. Unabridged digital audio book. 22 minutes.

Glossary

beasts (BEESTs) large animals or monsters with 4 legs

night vision (NYT VIH-zhuhn) the ability to see in darkness

pack (PAK) wolf family

quicksilver (KWIK-sil-vuhr) liquid mercury

shapeshifters (SHAYP-shif-tuhrs) creatures that can change their shapes

shift (SHIFT) to change

Index

Will silver kill a werewolf?
How does a person turn into a werewolf?

Books in the **Magic, Myth, and Mystery Express** series for young readers explore spooky creatures that go bump in the night, fill our dreams (or nightmares!), and make us afraid of the dark. Written with a high-interest level to appeal to a more mature audience, a lower level of complexity, and clear visuals, struggling readers can gain confidence.

BOOKS IN THIS SERIES

Discover Dragons	Discover Vampires
Discover Mermaids	Discover Werewolves
Discover Unicorns	Discover Zombies

45TH PARALLEL PRESS TITLES FEATURE:

High interest topics with accessible reading levels

Considerate vocabulary

Engaging content and fascinating facts

Clear text and formatting

Compelling photos

ISBN-13: 978-1668920701

9 781668 920701

45THPARALLELPRESS.COM

45TH PARALLEL PRESS